CW00950126

What Is
Psychotherapy?

What Is Psychotherapy?

The School of Life

Published in 2018 by The School of Life
70 Marchmont Street, London WC1N 1AB
Copyright © The School of Life 2018
Designed and typeset by Marcia Mihotich
Printed in Latvia by Livonia Print

A proportion of this book has appeared online at
www.theschooloflife.com/thebookoflife/

Every effort has been made to contact the copyright holders of
the material reproduced in this book. If any have been
inadvertently overlooked, the publisher will be pleased to make
restitution at the earliest opportunity.

The School of Life offers programmes, publications and
services to assist modern individuals in their quest to live more
engaged and meaningful lives. We've also developed a collection
of content-rich, design-led retail products to promote useful
insights and ideas from culture.

www.theschooloflife.com

ISBN 978-1-9997471-7-6

10 9 8 7 6 5 4 3

Contents

I

Introduction

Psychotherapy is one of the most valuable inventions of the last one hundred years, with an exceptional power to raise our levels of emotional well-being, improve our relationships, redeem the atmosphere in our families and assist us in mining our professional potential.

However, psychotherapy is also profoundly misunderstood and the subject of a host of unhelpful fantasies, hopes and suspicions. Its logic is rarely explained and its voice seldom heard with sufficient directness.

This book attempts to explain psychotherapy: what the needs are in all of us to which it caters; the methods by which it addresses these needs; and what the outcome of a therapeutic intervention could ideally be.

The book reflects a fundamental belief of the School of Life that psychotherapy is the single greatest step any of us can take towards self-understanding and fulfilment. A course of therapy stands to render us slightly less angry, self-defeating, unconfident, lost and sad.

This is a guide to the purpose and meaning of psychotherapy.

II
Why We Need
Therapy

A primal
wound

The origins of our need for psychotherapy lie deep in our pasts. No one intends for this to happen, but somewhere in childhood, our trajectory towards emotional maturity will almost certainly have been impeded. Even if we were sensitively cared for and lovingly handled, we can be counted upon not to have passed through our young years without sustaining some kind of deep psychological injury – what we can term a 'primal wound'.

Childhood opens us up to emotional damage in part because, unlike all other living things, *Homo sapiens* have an inordinately long and structurally claustrophobic pupillage. A foal can stand up thirty minutes after it is born. By the age of eighteen, a human will have spent around 25,000 hours in the company of its parents. A female grouper mother will unsentimentally dump up to 100 million eggs a year in the sandy banks off the north Atlantic seaboard, then swim away without seeing a single one of her offspring again. Even the blue whale, the largest animal on the planet, is sexually mature and independent by the age of five.

But for our part, we dither and linger. It can be a year until we take our first steps and two before we can speak in whole sentences. It is close to two decades before we are categorised as adults. In the meantime, we are at the mercy of that highly peculiar and distorting institution we call home, and its even more distinctive overseers, our parents.

Across the long summers and winters of childhood, we are intimately shaped by the ways of the big people around us: we come to know their favourite expressions, their habits, how they respond to a delay, the way they address us when they're cross. We know the atmosphere of home on a bright July morning and in the afternoon downpours of mid-April. We memorise the textures of the carpets and the smells of the clothes cupboards. As adults, we can still recall the taste of a particular biscuit we liked to eat after school and know intimately the tiny sounds a mother or father will make as they concentrate on an article in the newspaper. We can return to our original home for a holiday when we are parents ourselves and find – despite our car, responsibilities and lined faces – that we are eight again.

During our elongated gestation, we are at first, in a physical sense, completely at the mercy of our caregivers.

We are so frail, we could be tripped up by a twig; the family cat is a tiger. We need help crossing the road, putting on our coat, writing our name.

Our vulnerability is also emotional. We can't begin to understand our strange circumstances: who we are; where our feelings come from; why we are sad or furious; how our parents fit into the wider scheme; why they behave as they do. We necessarily take what the big people around us say as an inviolable truth; we can't help but exaggerate our parents' role on the planet. We are condemned to be enmeshed in their attitudes, ambitions, fears and inclinations. Our upbringing is always particular and peculiar.

As children, we can brush off very little of this. We are without a skin. If a parent shouts at us, the foundations of the earth tremble. We cannot tell that some of the harsh words were not really meant, had their origins in a difficult day at work, or are the reverberations of the adult's own childhood; it feels as if an all-powerful, all-knowing giant has decided, for good (if unknown) reasons, that we are to be annihilated.

Nor can we understand, when a parent goes away for the weekend, or relocates to another country, that they didn't leave us because we did something wrong or because we are unworthy of their love, but because even adults aren't always in control of their own destinies.

If parents are in the kitchen raising their voices, it can seem as though these two people must hate one another inordinately. To children, an overheard altercation (with a slammed door and swear words) may feel catastrophic, as though everything safe will disintegrate. There is no evidence in the child's grasp that arguments are a normal part of relationships; that a couple may be committed to a life-long union and at the same time forcefully express a wish that the other go to hell.

Children are equally helpless before their parents' idiosyncratic ideologies. They can't understand that an insistence that they not mix with another family from school, or that they follow particular dress codes, or hate a given political party, or worry about dirt or being less than two hours early for a flight, represents a partial understanding of priorities and reality.

Children don't have a job. They can't go elsewhere. They have no extended social network. Even when things are going well, childhood is an open prison.

As a result of the peculiarities of the early years, we become distorted and unbalanced. Aspects within us start to develop in odd directions. We find that we can't easily trust, or become unusually scared around people who raise their voices, or can't tolerate being touched. No one needs to do anything particularly shocking, illegal, sinister or wicked to us for serious distortions to unfold. The causes of our primal wound are rarely outwardly dramatic, but their impact can often be momentous and long-lasting. Such is the fragility of childhood that nothing outwardly appalling need have happened to us for us to wind up profoundly scrambled.

We know this point from tragedy. In the tales of the Ancient Greeks, it is not enormous errors and slips that unleash drama; it is the tiniest, most innocent, errors. Terrible consequences unfurl from seemingly minor starting points. Our emotional lives are similarly tragic in structure. Everyone around us may have been trying to do their best with us as children, yet we have ended up now, as adults, nursing major hurts that ensure we are much less than we might have been.

We are reluctant historians of our emotional pasts.

Imbalances

As a result of our childhoods, we are unbalanced; over most issues, we tend to list excessively, like a sailing yacht in high wind, in one direction or another. We are too timid or too assertive; too rigid or too accommodating; too focused on material success or maddeningly lackadaisical. We are obsessively eager around sex or painfully wary and nervous in the face of our own erotic impulses. We are dreamily naive or sourly down to earth; we recoil from risk or embrace it recklessly; we are determined never to rely on anyone or are desperate for another to complete us; we are overly intellectual or unduly resistant to ideas.

The encyclopedia of emotional imbalances is a volume without end. What is certain is that these imbalances come at vast cost, rendering us less able to exploit our talents and opportunities, less able to lead satisfying lives and a great deal less fun to be around.

Yet because we are reluctant historians of our emotional pasts, we easily assume that our imbalances are things we could never change; that they are innate. It is just how we are made. We simply are people who micromanage, or can't get much pleasure out of sex, or scream when someone contradicts us, or run away from lovers who are too kind to us. It may not be easy, but nor is it alterable or up for enquiry.

The truth is likely to be more hopeful, although more challenging in the short term. Our imbalances are invariably responses to something that happened in the past. We are a certain way because a primal wound knocked us off a more fulfilling trajectory years ago. In the face of a viciously competitive parent, we took refuge in underachievement. Having lived around a parent disgusted by the body, sex became frightening. Surrounded by material unreliability, we had to overachieve around money and social prestige. Hurt by a dismissive parent, we fell into patterns of emotional avoidance. A volatile parent pushed us towards our present meekness and inability to make a fuss. Early overprotectiveness inspired timidity and, around any complex situation, panic. A continually busy, inattentive parent was the catalyst for a personality marked by exhausting attention-seeking behaviour.

There is always a logic and always a history.

We can tell that our imbalances date from the past because they reflect the way of thinking and instincts of the children we once were. Without anything pejorative being meant by this, our way of being unbalanced tends towards a fundamental immaturity, bearing the marks of what was once a young person's attempt to grapple with something beyond their capacities.

When they suffer at the hands of an adult, children almost invariably take what happens to them as a reflection of something that must be wrong with them. If someone humiliates, ignores or hurts them, it must be because they are imbecilic, repugnant and worth neglecting. It can take many years, and a lot of patient inner exploration, to reach an initially less plausible conclusion: that the hurt was undeserved and that there were many other things going on, off-stage, in the raging adult's interior life for which the child was blameless.

Similarly, because children cannot easily leave a difficult situation, they are prey to powerful, limitless longings to fix the broken person they depend on. In the infantile imagination, it becomes the child's responsibility to mend all the anger, addiction or sadness of the grown-up they adore. It may be the work of decades to develop a wiser power to feel sad about, rather than eternally responsible for, those we cannot change, and perhaps to move on.

Communication patterns are beset by comparable childhood legacies. When something is wrong, children have no innate capacity to explain their cause. They lack the confidence, poise and verbal dexterity to get their points across with the calm and authority required. They tend to dramatic overreactions instead: insisting, nagging, exploding, screaming. Or, conversely, to excessive underreactions: sulking, sullenness, silence, avoidance. We may be well into middle age before we can shed our first impulses to explode at or flee from those who misunderstand our needs and more carefully and serenely try to explain them instead.

It is another feature of the emotional wounds of childhood that they tend to provoke what are in effect large-scale generalisations. Our wounds may have occurred in highly individual contexts: with one particular adult who hit their particular partner late at night in one particular terraced house in one particular town in the north. Or the wound may have been caused by one specific parent who responded with intense contempt after one specific job loss from one specific factory. But these events give rise to expectations of other people and of life more broadly. We grow to expect that everyone will become violent, that every partner will turn on us, and that every money problem will unleash depression and then abandonment. The character traits and mentalities that were formed in response to one or two central actors of childhood become our templates for interpreting pretty much anyone. For example, the always jokey and slightly manic way of being that we evolved to keep a listless mother engaged becomes our second nature. Even when she is long gone, we remain people who need to shine at every meeting, who require a partner to be continually focused on us, and who cannot listen to negative or dispiriting information of any kind. We are living the wide-open present through the narrow drama of the past.

Similarly, a childhood craving to pacify and never bother two squabbling, unhappy parents can far outlast our actual presence in their company. Decades later, we may still harbour a powerful desire to evade all confrontation, even though the original source of our hesitancy has long disappeared and such avoidance bears a heavy price.

It is a complicating factor that our imbalances don't cleanly reveal their origins – either to our own minds or to the world at large. We aren't really sure why we run away, get angry, have a proud and haughty air, miss every deadline, or cling excessively to people we love. Because the sources of our imbalances escape us, we miss out on garnering important sources of possible sympathy. The world judges us on the behaviours that our wounds inspire, rather than on the wounds themselves. The damage may have begun with a feeling of invisibility – a poignant enough phenomenon – but to a world that doesn't care to know more, we now come across as somewhat sickening show-offs. Maybe the damage began with being let down, but now we simply appear crazily controlling. Perhaps it started with a bullying, competitive father; now it seems as if we are just spineless.

We make our lives tougher than they should be because we insist on thinking of people as inept and mean rather than (as is usually the case) victims of what we have all travelled through: a tricky early history.

Amnesia and denial

What happened to us in childhood is the single greatest cause of how we function emotionally as adults. Therefore, what is surprising and unfortunate is how little of the past we can properly remember. We can recall the basic facts and a few incidents, but in terms of grasping in detail, with visceral emotion, how our present is influenced by the personalities and circumstances of our early years, we are often novices or simply sceptical as to the point of a close look backwards. In many cases, it would not be too strong to speak of willed amnesia.

The tendency to forget the primal wound of childhood is not hard to understand. It is implausible, but also humiliating, to imagine that events from so long ago might influence the bulk of our feelings and actions in the present. Blunt and clichéd-sounding psychological determinism negates our hopes for a life of dignified adult liberty. It seems crushing and, from certain perspectives, plain daft to suppose that our personalities might remain forged by incidents that unfolded before our fifth birthday. We would like to make sense of our moods in terms of what is happening in the present. If we feel angry with someone, we would like the cause to lie with them, rather than something three decades ago that has made us especially prone to taking offence.

We tend to adopt a sentimental attitude towards the past that is far more attentive to the occasional endearing exception than the more challenging norm. Family photos, almost always snapped at the happier moments, guide the process. There is much more likely to be an image of one's mother by the pool smiling with the expression of a giddy young girl than of her slamming the back door in rage at the misery of her marriage; there will be a shot of one's father genially performing a card trick, but no visual record of his long, brutal mealtime silences. A lot of editing goes on, encouraged by all sides.

With age, we naturally look at the world through the eyes of an adult rather than try to recover the distinctive and peculiar perspective of a child. To any grown-up, it is obvious that a three-year-old having a tantrum in a restaurant is to be condemned as irritating, theatrical and bad-mannered. But that is chiefly because we lack the encouragement or empathy to try to recreate the strange inner world of a small person (an inner world that was once our own) in which she might feel tired and bewildered, fearful that an unfamiliar dish is going to be forced on her, or lonely and humiliated by being the smallest person in a large and lugubrious dining room, far from her toy rabbit, left by mistake in the room upstairs.

When an adult locks a kitchen door to ensure silence during an hour-long business call, it is far from normal to picture the scene from the viewpoint of the very young child on the other side of the door, for whom this endless exclusion may seem proof that everything good and kind has mysteriously and suddenly died. It becomes difficult for us to keep in mind how much in all our characters was marked by what are (from a grown-up perspective) almost laughably minor yet hugely potent incidents.

It is not simply that we have forgotten the past. We could in principle re-enter the emotional spaces we once inhabited. It is for deeper reasons that we push aside the memories and actively restrict reflection on our histories.

We keep away from ourselves because so much of what we could discover threatens to be painful. We might discover that we were furious with, and resentful about, certain people we were only meant to love. We might discover how much ground there was to feel inadequate and guilty

27

on account of the many errors and misjudgements we have made. We might find that, although we wanted to be decent, law-abiding people, we harboured fantasies that went in deviant and aberrant directions. We might recognise how much was nauseatingly compromised and needed to be changed about our relationships and careers.

We not only have a lot to hide, we are liars of genius. It is part of the human tragedy that we are such natural self-deceivers. Our techniques are multiple and close to invisible.

We become addicted. Not to heroin or whisky, but to innocuous, everyday activities that attract no alarm or suspicion. We become addicted to checking the news or tidying the house, exercising or taking on fresh projects at work. To the world, it can look as if we are just being productive, but the clue to our compulsiveness lies in our motives. We are checking the news to keep the news from ourselves at bay; we are working for the company as an alternative to working on our soul. What properly indicates addiction is not what someone is doing, but their way of doing it to avoid encounters with themselves. We are addicts whenever we develop a manic reliance on something – anything – to keep our darker and more unsettling feelings at bay.

We lie by being very cheerful. It seems almost imperceptible from happiness. But with its remorseless and insistent upbeat quality, aggressive jolliness has very little to do with true satisfaction. The jollier doesn't just want the mood to be happy; they can't tolerate that it might in any way be sad, so unexplored and potentially overwhelming are their own background feelings of disappointment and grief.

We lie by attacking and denigrating what we love, but haven't managed to get. We dismiss the people we once wanted as friends, the careers we hoped one day to have, the lives we tried to emulate. We reconfigure what a desired but painfully elusive goal meant to us in the hope of not needing to register its loss properly.

We lie through a generalised cynicism, which we direct at everything and everyone so as to ward off misery about one or two things in particular. We say that all humans are terrible and every activity is compromised so that the specific cause of our pain does not attract scrutiny and feelings of shame.

We lie by filling our minds with impressive ideas, which blatantly announce our intelligence to the world but

We not only
have a lot
to hide,
we are liars
of genius.

subtly ensure we won't have much room left to rediscover the long-distant feelings of ignorance or confusion upon which the development of our personalities may rest.

We write dense books on the role of government bonds in the Napoleonic wars or publish extensively on Chaucer's influence on the mid-19th-century Japanese novel. We secure degrees from Institutes of Advanced Study or positions on editorial boards of scientific journals. Our minds are crammed with arcane data. We can wittily inform a dining table of guests who wrote the Enchiridion (Epictetus) or the life and times of Dōgen (the founder of Zen Buddhism). But we don't remember much about how life was long ago, back in the old house, when father left, mother stopped smiling and our trust broke in pieces.

We deploy knowledge and ideas that carry prestige to stand guard against the emergence of more humble but essential knowledge from our emotional past. We bury our personal stories beneath an avalanche of expertise. The possibility of a deeply consequential intimate enquiry is deliberately left to seem feeble and superfluous next to the supposedly grander task of addressing a conference on the political strategies of Dona Maria the First or the lifecycle of the Indonesian octopus.

We lean on the glamour of being learned to make sure we won't need to learn too much that hurts.

We lie by pretending that we are simpler than we really are and that too much psychology might be fuss and nonsense. We lean on a version of robust common sense to ward off intimations of our own awkward complexity. We imply that not thinking very much is evidence of a superior kind of intelligence.

In company, we deploy bluff strategies of ridicule against more complex accounts of human nature. We sideline avenues of personal investigation as unduly fancy or weird, implying that to lift the lid on inner life could never be fruitful or respectable. We use the practical mood of 9am Monday morning to ward off the complex insights of 3am the previous night, when the entire fabric of our existence came into question against the backdrop of a million stars, spread like diamonds on a mantle of black velvet. Deploying an attitude of vigorous common sense, we strive to make our moments of radical disquiet seem like aberrations rather than the central occasions of insight they might actually be.

We appeal to the understandable longing that our personalities are non-tragic, simple and easily comprehended so as to reject the stranger, but more useful, facts of our true, intricate selves.

A defence of emotional honesty has nothing to do with high-minded morality. It is ultimately cautionary and egoistic. We need to tell ourselves a little more of the truth because we pay too high a price for our lies. Through our deceptions, we cut ourselves off from possibilities of growth. We shut off large portions of our minds and end up uncreative, tetchy and defensive, while others around us have to suffer our irritability, gloom, manufactured cheerfulness or defensive rationalisations. Our neglect of the awkward sides of ourselves buckles our very being, emerging as insomnia or impotence, stuttering or depression; revenge for all the thoughts we have been so careful not to have. Self-knowledge is not a luxury so much as a precondition for a measure of sanity and inner comfort.

The emotionally
healthy childhood

We can sometimes be so modest about our power to know what might be good for others or ourselves, we forget it might be possible to hazard generalisations about what constitutes an emotionally healthy childhood. It can't be idiosyncracy or good luck; there are distinct themes and goals to identify. With a map of optimal development in mind, we could more clearly appreciate where dislocation begins, what we have to be grateful for, and what there is to regret. At a collective level, we could have more of a sense of what there is to achieve to generate a more emotionally privileged and therefore slightly saner world.

In the course of an emotionally healthy childhood, we could expect some of the following to occur.

Someone will put themselves profoundly at our service. If as adults we have even a measure of mental health, it is almost certainly because, when we were tiny, helpless infants, there was a person (to whom we essentially owe our lives) who pushed their needs aside for a time to focus wholly on our own. They interpreted what we could not say; they guessed what might be ailing us; they settled and consoled us. They kept the chaos and noise at bay and cut up the world into manageable pieces for us. They did not ask that we thank them, understand them or show them sympathy. They did not demand that we enquire how their day went or how they were sleeping at night. They treated us like royalty, so that we would later on be able to submit to the rigours and humiliations of an ordinary life. This temporarily one-sided relationship guaranteed our eventual ability to form a two-sided kind.

We may think of egoists as people who have grown sick from too much love. But the opposite is the case: an egoist is someone who has not yet had their fill. Self-centredness has to have a clean run in the early years if it isn't to haunt and ruin the later ones. The so-called narcissist is simply a benighted soul who has not had a chance to be inordinately and unreasonably admired at the start.

In an emotionally healthy childhood, someone is on hand to put the most positive spin on our behaviour. We are given the benefit of the doubt. We are assessed by what we might be one day, not by what we are right now. Someone is kind.

A harsh judge, for example, might say that we were 'attention-seeking'. Our caregiver imagines that what we most need is a hug and some encouraging words. We might have acted meanly. Our caregiver adds that we must have been feeling threatened. It looked as if we were negligent; the caregiver remembers that tiredness could have explained it.

Our carer constantly searches beneath the surface for more sympathetic explanations. They help us to be on our own side, to like ourselves, and therefore not to be too defensive about our flaws, the existence of which we grow strong enough to accept.

In a good childhood, the relationship with our caregiver is steady, consistent and long-term. We trust that they will be there tomorrow and the day after. They aren't volatile or fragile. They are almost boringly predictable and happy to be taken for granted. As a result, we develop a trust in relationships that spreads throughout our life. We are able to believe that what has gone well once can go well again and let such an expectation govern our choice of adult partners. We aren't mesmerised by people who are off-hand and unreliable; we don't relish being punished. We can pick out candidates who are kind and nurturing, and don't judge them as weak or deficient for being so.

If trouble strikes with our kindly partners, we don't panic anxiously or avoidantly turn away. We can confidently set about trying to repair a love we know we deserve.

In an emotionally healthy upbringing, we aren't always required to be wholly good boys or girls. We are allowed to get furious and sometimes revolting, at points to say 'absolutely not' and 'because I feel like it'. The adults know their own flaws and do not expect a child to be fundamentally better than they are. We do not have to comply at every turn to be tolerated. We can let others see our shadow sides.

This period of freedom prepares us one day to submit to the demands of society without having to rebel in self-defeating ways (rebels being, at heart, people who have had to obey too much too early). We can knuckle down and tow the line when it's in our long-term interest to do so. At the same time, we're not overly cowed or indiscriminately obedient either. We find a sound middle point between slavish compliance and self-destructive defiance.

In an emotionally healthy home, our carer isn't jealous of or competitive with us. They can allow themselves to be overtaken and superseded. They have had their moment in the limelight, or else are having it elsewhere beyond the family. They can be proud rather than rivalrous of the achievements of the (usually same-sex) child. It doesn't need to be all about them.

The good carer isn't overly ambitious on the child's behalf. They want them to do well, but for their own sake, and in their own way. There is no particular script that the offspring has to follow to be loved; the child isn't required to support the carer's frayed self-belief or burnish their image in the eyes of the world.

In an emotionally healthy upbringing, the child learns that things that break can be fixed. Plans can go awry, but new ones can be made. The carer models for the child how to calm down, plough on and remain hopeful. A voice of resilience, originally external, becomes the way the child learns to speak to themselves. There are alternatives to panic.

Importantly, plenty goes wrong in the emotionally healthy childhood. No one has staked their reputation on rendering the whole thing perfect. The carer does not see it as their role to remove every frustration. They intuit that a lot of good comes from having the right, manageable

Plenty goes wrong in the emotionally healthy childhood.

kind of friction, through which the child develops their own resources and individuality. In contact with bearable disappointment, the child is prompted to create their own internal world, in which they can dream, hatch fresh plans, self-soothe and build up their own resources.

The child can see that the good carer is neither entirely good nor wholly bad, and therefore is worthy of neither idealisation nor denigration. The child accepts the faults and virtues of the carer with melancholy maturity and gratitude and thereby, by extension, becomes ready to accept that everyone they like will be a mixture of positive and negative. As adults, they won't fall deeply in love and then become furious at the first moment of let-down. They have a realistic sense of what can be expected of life alongside another good enough human.

Soberingly, despite all our advances in technology and material resources, we are not much more advanced in the art of delivering emotionally healthy childhoods than previous generations. The number of breakdowns, inauthentic lives and broken souls shows no marked signs of decline. We are failing to offer one another tolerable childhoods not because we are evil or indifferent but because we still have so far to go before we know how to do that most apparently simple yet infinitely complicated of things: love.

The tool that might just get us there is psychotherapy.

The markers of
emotional health

One way to start assessing how badly we have been knocked by our early years – and where we might therefore need to direct most of our repair work and attention – is to identify a range of markers of emotional health and imagine how we fare in relation to them. At least four markers suggest themselves.

1. Self-love

Self-love is the quality that determines how much we can be friends with ourselves and remain on our own side.

When we meet a stranger who has things we don't, how quickly do we feel ourselves pitiful, and how long can we remain assured by the decency of what we have and are? When another person frustrates or humiliates us, can we let the insult go, able to perceive the senseless malice beneath the attack, or are we left brooding and devastated, implicitly identifying with the verdict of our enemies? How much can the disapproval or neglect of public opinion be offset by the memory of the steady attention of a few significant people in the past?

In relationships, do we have enough self-love to leave an abusive union? Or are we so down on ourselves that we carry an implicit belief that harm is all we deserve? In a different vein, how good are we at apologising to a lover for things that might be our fault? How rigidly self-righteous do we need to be? Can we dare to admit mistakes, or does an admission of guilt or error bring us too close to a background sense of nullity?

In the bedroom, how clean and natural or alternatively disgusting and sinful do our desires feel? Might they be a little odd, but not bad or dark, since they emanate from within us and we are not wretches?

At work, do we have a reasonable, well-grounded sense of our worth, and so feel able to ask for (and expect to get) the rewards we are due? Can we resist the need to please others indiscriminately? Are we sufficiently aware of our genuine contribution to say no?

2. Candour

Candour determines the extent to which difficult ideas and troubling facts can be consciously admitted into the mind, soberly explored and accepted without denial.

How much can we admit to ourselves about who we are – even if, or especially when, the matter is unpleasant? How much do we need to insist on our own normality and wholehearted sanity? Can we explore our own minds and look into their darker and more troubled corners without flinching too much? Can we admit to folly, envy, sadness and confusion?

Around others, how ready are we to learn? Do we need always to take a criticism of one part of us as an attack on everything about us? How ready are we to listen when valuable lessons come in painful guises?

3. Communication

Can we patiently and reasonably put our disappointments into words that, more or less, enable others to see our point? Or do we internalise pain, act it out symbolically or discharge it with counterproductive rage?

When other people upset us, do we feel we have the right to communicate or must we slam doors and retreat into sulks? When the desired response isn't forthcoming, do we ask others to guess what we have been too angrily panicked to spell out? Or can we have a plausible second

How ready
are we to
listen when
valuable lessons
come in painful
guises?

go and take seriously the thought that others are not merely being nasty in misunderstanding us? Do we have the inner resources to teach rather than insist?

4. Trust

How risky is the world? How readily might we survive a challenge in the form of a speech, a romantic rejection, a bout of financial trouble, a journey to another country or a common cold? How close are we, at any time, to catastrophe? What material are we made of?

Will new acquaintances like us or wound us? If we are a touch assertive, will they take it or collapse? Will unfamiliar situations end in a debacle? Around love, how tightly do we need to cling? If our lover is distant for a while, will they return? How controlling do we need to be? Can we approach an interesting-looking stranger? Or move on from an unsatisfying relationship?

Overall, do we feel the world to be wide, safe and reasonable enough for us to have a legitimate shot at contentment, or must we settle, resentfully, for inauthenticity and misunderstanding?

It isn't our fault (or, in a sense, anyone else's) that many of these questions are so hard to answer in the affirmative. But, by entertaining them, we are at least starting to know what kind of shape our wounds have and, therefore, what kind of bandages might be necessary.

III
How Therapy
Works

Psychotherapy is a tool; like all tools, it has been designed to help us overcome an inborn weakness and to extend our capacities beyond those with which nature originally endowed us. In this sense, it is not metaphysically different from a bucket, which remedies our problems of holding water in our palms, or a knife, which makes up for the bluntness of our teeth.

What is distinctive about therapy is what it is a tool for: it is an invention to help improve the way our emotions operate. It has been devised to correct the otherwise substantial difficulties we face in understanding ourselves, trusting others, communicating successfully, honouring our potential and feeling adequately serene, confident, authentic, direct and unashamed.

For such an important invention, psychotherapy is low on overt signs of innovation. Technically speaking, it requires only a comfortable room free of any interruptions, fifty minutes, possibly twice a week for a year or so, two chairs and some chat. But at the level of training, the psychotherapist needs to undertake a period of extensive education in the workings of the mind, which – in the more responsible jurisdictions – has some of the rigour, intellectual ambition and periods of hands-on experience demanded by the acquisition of a pilot's licence.

To deliver on its promises, psychotherapy relies on at least eight distinct moves.

1
Witnessing

Most of what we are remains a secret to the world, because we appreciate how much of it flouts the laws of decency and sobriety by which we would like to live. We know that we would not last long in society if a stream of raw data ever leaked out of our minds.

A lot of what is inside us can seem daft: how we felt a strange impulse to burst into tears when reading a children's book about an elephant befriending a baby sparrow; how often we imagine acquiring a power to go back in time and correct the missed opportunities of our adolescence. From a harsh angle, some of what is inside is distinctly pathetic: how worried we are about asking where the bathroom is; how envious we are of a close acquaintance; how much we worry about our hair. A significant part is alarming and quasi-illegal: our fantasies about a work colleague and a family member; our plans for what we would ideally do to an enemy.

In response to our isolation, we are often told about the importance of friends. But we know that the tacit contract of any friendship is that we will not bother the incumbent with more than a fraction of our madness. A lover is another solution, but it is not in the remit of any partner to delve into, and accept, more than a modest share of what we are.

In every social interaction, we sensibly ensure that there remains a large and secure divide between what we say to people and what is truly going on inside our minds.

The exception lies with psychotherapy. Here, remarkably, we can say pretty much anything we want – and, indeed, should strive to do so. We don't have to impress the therapist or reassure them of our sanity. We need to tell them what is going on. There is no need to stop them thinking we are perverted, odd or terrified. We can gingerly hint at some very dark things about us and will find that our interlocutor is not horrified or offended but only calmly interested. We will learn that we are not monsters or freaks. We arrive at the opposite of loneliness.

2
Worldliness

Therapists know a lot about the unvarnished truths of human nature. They have close-up experience of the greatest traumas – incest and rape, suicide and depression – as well as the smaller pains and paradoxes: a longing provoked by a glance at a person in a library that took up the better part of twenty years; an otherwise gentle soul who broke a door; a handsome, athletic man who can no longer perform.

They know that inside every adult there remains a child who is confused, angry, hurt and longing to have their say and their reality recognised. They appreciate that this child has to get to know itself again and will want to be heard, perhaps through tears or near-incomprehensible mutterings, which might be at odds with the surface maturity and self-command normally associated with grown-ups.

Therapists have sufficiently acclimatised themselves to the reality of what people are like not to need to censor or deliver moralistic judgements. They have done this not primarily through books, but by being courageous about knowing their own nature. They may not share our fantasies exactly, but they accept that their own are as colourful and as complex. They don't have our precise anxieties, but they know well enough the powerful and peculiar fears that hold us all hostage.

They can start to help us because they have an accurately broad grasp of what it means to be normal – which is, of course, so far from what we insist on pretending is normal. They don't require us to be conventionally good or typical to shore up their fragile sense of self or of reality. Their only requirement is that we admit, without too much defensiveness, to some of what is going on inside us.

Therapists
have an
accurately
broad grasp
of what it
means to be
normal.

3
Kindness

Therapists are, very gratifyingly, on our side. Without ill intention, most people are not particularly; they are intermittently jealous, bored, vindictive, keen to prove a point or distracted by their own lives. But the therapist brings a focused, generous attention to our case. Their room is safe and set aside from day-to-day pressures. They are sorry that we have suffered. They understand that it must have been worrying, enraging or exciting. They know we didn't do it on purpose or that we had our reasons if we did. Without flattering us in a rote way, merely because it is their job to do so, they strive to enter into our experience and to side with it. They look at reality through our eyes so as to start correcting a legacy of shame and isolation.

At the same time, their kindness makes ours a little less necessary. Normal life requires that we constantly weigh the impact of our words on other people. We have to consider their priorities, ask how their children are, and hold their concerns in mind.

Here there is no such call. Like a parent who doesn't need

a small child to reciprocate, the therapist voluntarily foregoes equality in the relationship; they won't talk of their regrets or insist on their anecdotes. They simply want to help us find what is best for us, understood on our terms. They won't have a preconceived view of how we are meant to live, just a great deal of sympathy for the complexities and the suffering we have endured already, and a desire to help us with the future.

That said, kindness is not merely pleasant. Knowing that we have someone on our side is designed to lend us the courage to face up to experiences we normally evade. In a sufficiently calm, reassuring and interested environment, we can look at areas of vulnerability we otherwise lack the courage to tackle. We can dare to think that perhaps we were wrong or that we have been angry for long enough, that it might be best to outgrow our justifications or cease trying to seduce every audience.

The kindness of another person gives us the security needed to probe constructively at our clever, puzzling, evasive minds.

4
Listening

One of the structural flaws of these minds is that it is immensely hard for us to think deeply and coherently for any length of time. We keep losing the thread. Competing, irrelevant ideas have a habit of flitting across the mental horizon and scrambling our tentative insights. Every now and then, consciousness inexplicably goes blank for a moment. Left to our own devices, we quickly start to doubt the value of what we are trying to make sense of, and can experience overpowering urges to check the news or search out a biscuit. As a result, some of the topics we most need to examine – where our relationship is going; what we might do next at work; how we should best answer a letter; what bothers us so much about the way our partner returns our hand after an attempt at a caress – founder into the mental sands, to our grave psychological cost.

What helps enormously in our attempts to know our own minds is, surprisingly, the presence of another mind. For all the glamour of the solitary seer, thinking usually happens best in tandem. The curiosity of someone else gives us the confidence to remain curious about the thickets of our own minds. It is the application of a light pressure from outside us that firms up the jumbled impressions that lie within. The requirement to verbalise our intimations mobilises our flabby reserves of concentration.

Occasionally a friend might be unusually attentive and ready to hear us out. But it isn't enough for them merely to be quiet. The highest possibilities of listening extend far beyond the polite fact of not being interrupted. To really be heard means being the recipient of a strategy of 'active listening'.

From the start, the therapist will use a succession of very quiet but significant prompts to help us develop and stick to the points we are circling. These suggest that there is no hurry but that someone is there, following every utterance. At strategic points, the therapist will drop in a mission-critical and hugely benign 'do say more' or an equally powerful 'go on'. Therapists are experts of the low-key positive sound: the benevolent, nuanced 'ahh' and the potent 'mmm', two of the most significant noises in the aural repertoire of psychotherapy that together invite us to remain faithful to what we were starting to say, however peculiar.

As beneficiaries of active listening, our ideas, memories and concerns don't have to fall into neat, well-formed sentences. We are allowed to stumble and get confused. But the active listener contains and gardens the emerging confusion. They gently take us back over ground we covered too quickly and prompt us to address a salient point that we might have sidestepped; they will help us chip away at an agitating issue while continually reassuring us that what we are saying is valuable. All the while, they will note minor changes in our facial expressions and tone of voice. They will be interested in the way we choose our words, and attentive not only to what we actually express but to how we might otherwise have put it.

They do not treat us like unusually unsophisticated beings or strangely ineffective communicators; they are simply immensely alive to how difficult it is for anyone to piece together and express what they really have on their minds.

5
Time

Therapy is built on the understanding that we will not be able to transmit our key experiences in one or two self-contained blocks of time. We live in time and have to decode ourselves in time. We can't be in all the moods we need to access on every occasion. Some weeks will find us readier than others to investigate particular memories or consider certain viewpoints. The therapist allows us to start the conversation anywhere we want, permits us to wander through our internal corridors, confident that so long as we keep showing up and sharing, we will eventually drop enough clues to assemble a psychological portrait of the self, like an ancient vase slowly being pieced together from fragments sifted from mounds of debris.

6
Interpretation

The therapist's active listening is not meandering: what underpins it is an attempt to understand – for our sake – what the subterranean operations of the past are doing to the present.

We arrive in therapy with questions. We have a presenting problem that hints at, but does not fully capture, the origins of our suffering. Why, for instance, do we repeatedly fall for people who attempt to control and humiliate us? How can we be both so convinced we need to leave a job and yet have remained resolutely unable to locate a more satisfying replacement? Why are we paralysed by anxiety in every public context? Why do we sabotage sexual possibility?

By their questions and their attention, their careful probing and investigative stealth, the therapist tries – harder than anyone has probably yet done – to discover how our presenting problem might be related to the rest of our existence and, in particular, the turmoils of childhood. Over many sessions, a succession of small discoveries contributes to an emerging picture of the sources of our emotional wounds, and of the way in which our character slowly evolved in response to them in a way that hampers our possibilities today.

We may, for example, start to sense how a feeling of rivalry with a parent led us to retire early from workplace challenges in order to hold on to their love, as well as seeing, perhaps for the first time, that the logic of our self-sabotage no longer holds. Or we might perceive the way an attitude of aggressive cynicism, which restricts our personalities and our friendships, might have had its origins in a parent who let us down at a time when we could not contain our vulnerability, and thereby turned us into people who try at every juncture to disappoint themselves early and definitively rather than allowing the world to mock our emerging hopes at a time of its own choosing.

It is unhelpful to state any of this too starkly or harshly. An interpretation delivered in its bare bones will be anticlimactic and bathetic and most likely prompt resistance or aggression. For the interpretation to work its effect, we as clients need to move from merely assenting to it intellectually to having an internal experience of the emotions it refers to. We need to feel for ourselves (rather than take on trust) the continued presence, within our adult selves, of the poignantly susceptible person we once were.

For the process to work, the therapist must tactfully let it seem as if the discovery of the structure of our troubles is almost entirely our own unhurried work.

7
A relationship

The ongoing contact between ourselves and the therapist, the weekly sessions that may continue over months or years, contribute to the creation of something that sounds, in a professional context, distinctly odd: a relationship.

We are almost certain to have come to see a therapist in the first place because, in some way, having relationships has become beset with difficulties that we sense, but don't quite understand: maybe we try to please people at once, secure their admiration, but then feel inauthentic and inwardly numb and pull back. Perhaps we fall in love very powerfully, but then always discover a major flaw in a partner that puts us off and makes us end the story and restart the cycle.

The relationship with our therapist may have little in common with the sort of unions we have in ordinary life. We won't ever be shopping together or watching TV side by side in bed. But, unavoidably and conveniently, we bring to our encounters with the therapist the very tendencies that emerge in our relations with other people in our lives. Here too we may be seductive but then cold,

The therapeutic relationship acts as a microcosm of our relationships in general.

or prone to idealisation then seized by an impulse to flee. Except that now, in the presence of the therapist, our tendencies will have a chance to be witnessed, slowed down, discussed, sympathetically explored and – in their more damaging manifestations – overcome. The relationship with the therapist becomes a litmus test of one's behaviour with people more generally and thereby allows us, on the basis of greater self-awareness, to modify and improve how we relate to others.

In the therapy room, our proclivities and habits are noticed and can be commented on, not as reproaches but as important information about our character that we deserve to become aware of. The therapist will (with kindness) point out that we're reacting as if we had been attacked, when they only asked a question; they might draw our attention to how readily we seem to want to tell them impressive things about our finances (yet they like us anyway), or how we seem to rush to agree with them when they're only trying out an idea of which they themselves are not very sure. They will signal where we are prone to pin to them attitudes or outlooks that they don't actually have. They may note how invested we seem to be in the idea that they are disappointed in us, or find us boring or are revolted by our sexuality. They will point out our habit of casting people in the present in roles that must derive from the past and will search with us for the origins of these attributions, which are liable to mimic what we felt towards influential caregivers and now shape what we expect from everyone.

The therapeutic relationship acts as a microcosm of our relationships in general and so can be used as a unique vehicle for learning about our more imperceptible emotional tendencies. By re-experiencing relational problems with an empathetic other who will not respond as ordinary people will, who will not shout at us, complain, say nothing or run away, we can be helped to understand what we are up to and given a chance to let new patterns of relating emerge.

The relationship with the therapist becomes a template for how we might form relationships with others going forward, freed from the manoeuvres and background assumptions that we carried within us from childhood, and that can impede us so grievously in the present.

The therapeutic relationship may be for us the first properly healthy relationship we have had, one in which we learn to hold off from imposing our assumptions on the other and trust them enough to let them see the larger, more complex reality of who we are, without too much intervening shame or embarrassment. It becomes a model – earned in a highly unusual situation – that we start to apply in the more humdrum but consequential setting of daily life, with our friends and our partners.

8
Inner voices

Somewhere in our minds, removed from the day to day, there sits a judge. They watch what we do, study how we perform, examine the effect we have on others, track our successes and failures – and then, eventually, they pass a verdict. The origins of the voice of the inner judge is simple to trace: it is an internalisation of the voice of people who were once outside us. We absorb the tones of contempt and indifference or of charity and warmth that we will have heard across our formative years. Sometimes, a voice is positive and benign, encouraging us to run those final few yards. More often, the inner voice is not nice at all. It is defeatist and punitive, panic-ridden and humiliating. It does not represent anything like our best insights or most mature capacities.

Part of what therapy offers us is a chance to improve how we judge ourselves and the voices we hear in our heads. It can involve learning – in a conscious, deliberate way – to speak to ourselves in the way the therapist spoke to us over many months. In the face of challenges, we can enquire of ourselves, 'And what would they say now?' After we have heard their constructive, kindly voice often enough and around tricky enough issues, it will come to feel like a natural response; eventually, it will become our own thoughts.

IV
Case Studies

One of the best ways to understand what psychotherapy involves is to read accounts of what happened to people when they went: the problems they came in with, the discussions that were had, and how things changed as a result. What follow are four representative case studies of the therapeutic process.

Underachievement

It ought to be a source of immense satisfaction for a parent to see their child secure success and esteem in their chosen career. In reality, this is only possible if the parent has learnt to be comfortable with being superseded by their child, if they have the inner resources not to mind surrendering leadership, if their own sense of self is robust. It is not enough to know how to feel tender around the helplessness of an infant; an equally crucial, though less recognised, challenge is to cope with their eventual strength as an adult.

Twenty-seven-year-old Nathan [not his real name] arrives in therapy complaining of a sense of listlessness and despair.

He had always seemed marked out for a special destiny. His father is one of the city's most powerful bankers, a self-made man who overcame a deprived childhood to achieve extraordinary wealth and renown. His mother, a former beauty queen, is on the board of the opera, the museum and several children's charities.

Nathan is their only son. There has long been a feeling that he would achieve something commensurate with the status of his parents. At a young age, his mother called him 'little genius'. Family friends would joke to his father that his son looked exactly like him (the resemblance is striking, even though the son retains a handsome head of hair) and would soon be one to watch in the trading world.

But none of the early promise has borne fruit. Nathan did not feel his grades in maths were good enough to follow his father into business. He was more naturally drawn to the arts and, after graduating, tried to write a novel. He kept at it for three years, but after yet another rejection letter he put the manuscript aside. He also started and abandoned three film scripts.

He complains about his love life. He is often in the role of pursuing women who want to be his friend but not his lover. Sex can be awkward.

Nathan is currently working in a basic administrative role in an art gallery in a run-down part of the city. His salary doesn't start to cover his rent, which is taken care of by his father. Payment involves a complex administrative rigmarole, in which Nathan is required to show up at his father's office every month with a receipt from the landlord and is asked by the PA to wait outside for up to an hour while his father finishes apparently urgent business inside.

Nathan calls himself, in a dry sardonic voice, with shoulders stooped, the ultimate loser.

On the surface, parents invariably speak of wanting the best for their child. But if they are nursing, somewhere within, a wound of neglect and humiliation, it may be intolerably envy-inducing to see a child succeed against odds smaller than those they had to endure.

The adult will feel compelled to keep winning, even against the child they ostensibly love: it might be at table tennis or Monopoly, in exam grades or political arguments. Or at life more generally. There is a basic sense that there cannot be two winners in the same household and that it is the senior party who has to triumph.

Nathan has always admired but been intimidated by his father. He mentions in an early therapy session that when he was no more than seven he tried to identify something to buy his father for his birthday but realised he would never be in a position to afford anything this potentate of finance actually needed.

He also remembers a time – the first and only time – he beat his father at tennis. They were at their house in the Bahamas. Nathan was fifteen. The father was proud of his game. But this time, Nathan won. Clearly and unambiguously. Yet the father accused Nathan of being a 'cheat' and stormed off the court in fury. They didn't speak all day, and never played again.

In the unconscious mind, a child facing parental competitiveness understands that they are being offered a deal: a choice between love and early retirement or success and possible expulsion. Unfortunately, it mostly doesn't feel like a choice. The capacity to stand up for oneself requires enough of an experience of unconditional love at the outset for the threat of its loss to seem endurable down the line. But without inner ballast, the child has no realistic way forward other than to put aside their ambitions and submit to (imperceptible and never quite stated) parental edicts.

For Nathan, the work of therapy involves seeing that his father's seeming support is really an expression of rivalry. His father is generous with money, but the way it is distributed serves to reinforce the idea of Nathan's dependent, inferior position.

At the same time as bringing the father's competitiveness to consciousness, therapy helps Nathan to appreciate its origins. The father is not so much vindictive as fragile. His power in the world is almost inversely proportionate to his feeling of inner security.

The more he dwells on his father's past, the more Nathan starts to feel sorry for, and almost protective of, him. It cannot be much fun to be an adult threatened by an adolescent's growing skill at backhand.

One way to meddle with the ambitions of a child is to imply that the child cannot be a success; the other, equally harmful way, is to insist that he or she must be one.

Nathan's mother's greatest wish had once been to study literature and become a university professor. It didn't happen.

She has always been extremely encouraging to Nathan – in a way. When he was little, he started reading early, which began her habit of referring to him as a genius. When he turned thirteen, she gave him the complete works of Nabokov. Now she sends him links to literary articles and talks about new novels that he must read. She took the rejection of her son's novel very badly – perhaps worse than Nathan himself did. She urges him to try again and to meet up with a creative writing teacher she met who has offered to help with plot structure. Nathan can't bear to tell her that he's thrown away his book and all its accompanying notes. He dreads that one day he will have to inform his mother of a greater truth: that he is not the genius she needed him to be.

It is as harmful to require a child to succeed as it is to require them to fail. In both cases, the child's true developmental needs are sacrificed to the parent's psychological requirements. Sincere love is neutral in this area; it doesn't mean needing someone either to succeed or to fail, but rather to grow on their own terms, which might be compatible with being either quite ordinary or, perhaps, exceptional.

In the course of a year of therapy, Nathan recognises that the world is broader and more robust than he had first imagined. A client of the gallery where he works offers him a new job in his architecture firm. Nathan accepts that he won't ever write a novel, and perhaps never even wanted to. This causes an uncomfortable lunch with his mother, but it's only one lunch.

Although it means dramatically tightening his expenditure, Nathan decides that he doesn't need his father's money for his rent. He tells him politely but firmly that he won't come uptown for another cheque. This creates an unexpected response. His father immediately offers to give him a large lump sum upfront, no questions asked. Nathan is grateful but hasn't touched the money yet.

At around the same time, he develops a new confidence around women, and meets a young German architect in the office. The sex is pretty good.

Step by step, Nathan is starting to discover something even more satisfying than knowing how to please his parents: leading his own life.

It is as
harmful to
require a child
to succeed
as it is to
require them
to fail.

The good child

We tend to assume that all is well with good children. They don't pose immediate problems; they keep their bedroom tidy, do their homework on time and are willing to help with the washing up. But the secret sorrows – and future difficulties – of the good child are tied to the fact that they behave this way not out of choice but because they feel under irresistible pressure to do so. They are trying to cope with a legacy of caregivers who had no capacity to deal with their more complicated, and inevitably darker, reality.

Eva works in a top law firm. She is hugely coveted and has been made a partner at the age of only thirty – an almost unparalleled achievement.

Eva comes to therapy because she recently collapsed on stage at a conference where she was delivering the keynote speech. This was hugely embarrassing but also deeply mysterious. The doctors could find nothing wrong. Eva interprets it as an almost deliberate act of self-sabotage. She registers an impulse in herself to let her firm down, to fail and mess up – like she has never done before.

Eva does not know where the impulse comes from but, after too long of being very good, she has an occasional and powerful longing to try to be bad. 'I wonder what it would be like to blow everything sky high,' she tells her therapist, with a burst of almost childlike glee, which she then quickly checks, feeling a need to reassure the therapist of her fundamentally law-abiding nature.

On one occasion, Eva rather enjoyed taking a day off work, pretending that she was ill in bed, and then spending many hours with a girlfriend at an upscale shopping mall instead. But she became terrified that wind of her 'bad behaviour' might reach her colleagues.

We imagine good children to be fine because they do everything that is expected of them. But the good child isn't good because, by a quirk of nature, they simply have no inclination to be anything else. They are good because they lack other options. Some good children are good out of love of a depressed, harassed parent who makes it clear they just can't cope with any more complications or difficulties. Others are good at soothing a violently angry parent who threatens to become catastrophically frightening at any sign of less than perfect conduct.

Eva's parents were immigrants. From the first, they instilled in her a ferocious work ethic. When Eva's father left the family, her mother had to support three children on her own. Eva was the oldest. She remembers hearing her mother wake up at 4am to start her first shift.

There was little room for laughter. Eva took school very seriously, was desperate to get good grades, and pulled herself through university, working in the evenings and at weekends in a care home. There has been a lot of disappointment in Eva's mother's life. Eva always struggled hard to ensure she would not be another.

Now her mother, who lives very near her, expects to hear every detail of her daughter's life and invariably has a lot of very firm advice about what Eva should do.

The repression of the good child's share of challenging emotions, although it produces short-term pleasant obedience, stores up enormous difficulty. The good child becomes a keeper of too many secrets and a poor communicator of unpopular but important things.

In one session, Eva arrives having cut her hair short, and shows the therapist a small new tattoo she has had done on her wrist. She is excited by these steps but nervous about the reaction her mother might have when she sees her at the weekend. The session focuses on how to understand her mother's worries. Eva's mother will think that it is impossible for Eva to be a partner in a law firm and have short hair or a discreet tattoo. These fears are exaggerated, of course, but her mother is trying to express as best she can her intense hopes for, and love of, her child. Her mother will be angry, but that's because she's frightened, she cares and she is sure that any indication of unorthodox behaviour will be catastrophically punished by the world. But with the therapist, Eva can consider the evidence: the law firm is quite conservative, but there's no reason to think that her new hairstyle will damage her career.

The trouble of the good child is that they have no experience of other people being able to tolerate, or remain calm in front of, their badness. They have missed out a vital privilege accorded to the healthy child: that of being able to display confident, envious, greedy or aggressive sides and yet be met with toleration and love nevertheless. Perhaps a rebellion isn't always easy for a resilient family, but, like a storm, everyone takes it in their stride.

The excessively good person typically has particular problems around sex. As a child, they may have been praised for being pure and innocent. As they become an adult, however, like all of us, they discover the ecstasies of sex, which can be beautifully perverse and excitingly disgusting – and radically at odds with what they believe is right. In response, they may disavow their desires, grow cold and detached from their bodies, or perhaps give in to their longings only in a disproportionate way that is destructive to other parts of their lives and leaves them disgusted and frightened.

Eva has not been in a sustained relationship. There have been people, both men and women, who she has really liked, but it's always been difficult when things become sexual. She becomes very wary and unresponsive. At work she has overheard people talking about 'the ice queen' and she is sure they were referring to her.

She has had some intense sexual encounters – once in the restroom of a restaurant – that she is deeply embarrassed to mention and that she describes as 'sordid'. They were with people she hardly knew, who she would 'never normally have anything to do with'.

It has been difficult for Eva to discuss her sexual fantasies in sessions; she was sure the therapist would be appalled by some of her 'perverted' imaginings. It took many months to reassure her that there was no surprise or horror at her revelations, and that someone could entirely respect her and also properly understand her sexual character. It had seemed to her impossible that anyone competent and decent could do both. This wasn't something she realised in one go; it took many re-encounters with the same anxiety for a degree of trust gradually to evolve.

Now Eva has become interested in finding someone 'for love and sex'. She is still looking, but she has recently had dates with a couple of people she loves talking to and with whom she can imagine having the kind of sex she really wants. It is still early days, but it no longer feels impossible.

Maturity involves a frank, unfrightened relationship with our own darkness, complexity and ambition. It involves accepting that not everything that makes us happy will please others or be honoured as especially 'nice' by society, but that it can be important to explore and hold on to it nevertheless. The desire to be good is one of the loveliest things in the world, but in order to have a genuinely good life, we may sometimes need to be (by the standards of the good child) fruitfully and bravely bad.

After a year in therapy, Eva has started to see less of her mother. She is genuinely grateful and considerate, but can politely yet firmly push back on her excessive demands to be informed about everything. The phrases 'I love you, but I can't see you on Sunday' and 'I love you, but I'm going to keep that one to myself' have been important to her: they put into words the idea that she can let her mother down in certain ways and still appreciate her mother's past efforts.

At work, Eva has had a fruitful, though tricky, confrontation with a senior partner: when a number of impossibly tight deadlines were imposed on her team, she was able to explain that they couldn't all be met; she couldn't be a good colleague simply by pretending that everything could be done; she could only do her job well by making a bit of a fuss and getting extra resources assigned to the project, even though that wasn't the answer her superiors wanted to hear.

Splitting

The pioneering mid-20th-century Viennese psychoanalyst Melanie Klein (1882–1960) drew attention to something dramatic that happens in the minds of babies during feeding sessions with their mothers. When feeding goes well, the baby is blissfully happy and sees their mother as 'good'. But if, for whatever reason, the feeding process is difficult, the baby can't grasp that it is dealing with the same person it liked a lot only a few hours ago.

Therefore, it splits off from the actual mother a second 'bad' version, whom it deems to be a separate, hateful individual, responsible for deliberately frustrating its wishes and, in the process, protecting the image of the good mother in its mind. In the baby's world, there is a 'good' mother who is ideally lovely and perfect and another 'bad' mother who is entirely horrible. When there is any difficulty, the baby feels that the 'bad' mother has turned up, and that if she could just be made to go away, by being annihilated or banished, the 'good' mother would come back and everything would be fine. This process is known in therapy as 'splitting'. It can cause us immense difficulties, and it doesn't just happen in babies.

Miriam is strikingly beautiful; she has a very engaging personality: open, direct and friendly. She has worked in various impressive roles around the media. She has an assured, cosmopolitan air. What has brought her to therapy is that for years she has been in a painful romantic cycle with men: she falls madly in love with someone wonderful, then, after around three months, and normally after a relatively small incident, she falls dramatically out of love with them again.

Miriam is savagely funny when she describes what turned out to be wrong with each of the men she's been out with. There was the fantastically 'anal' graphic designer who was obsessed with ironing his socks and underpants and who would 'practically froth at the mouth' if he discovered a fork in the knife section of the cutlery drawer. There was a Finnish filmmaker with a habit of going into extended monologues about (here she copies his accent) 'how he wanted to get back to the ways of the forest'. There was a banker who (she says) was in love with his own sister.

But behind the wit, there is a grim pattern: the people Miriam loves all turn out to be 'buffoons, narcissists, lost boys, scumbags, weirdos or maniacs – or some combination of them all.'

Ideally, over time, the child manages to put together the two images of their carer. Painfully, and with much constructive disappointment, they see that there aren't really two versions: there is just one person who is a bearable combination of nice and frustrating; who is delightful in some ways and a bit disappointing in others. If things go well, the child comes, sadly but realistically, to grasp that there is no ideal, 'perfect' mother, just one person who is usually lovely but can also be cross, busy, tired, who can make mistakes, and be very interested in other people. By extension, they see that this is how other people generally are. What look like failings are often tied to what is attractive about them: they are a bit fussy because they are so caring; they are a touch boring because they are serious about one or two things. In the best possible scenario, the child comes to be reconciled to reality, and able to love people as they are.

Miriam lost her father when she was young. She cherishes memories of him. He was great fun, clever and kind. She loved it when he took her swimming. He often read to her at night and put on different voices for all the characters. But she never discovered the full reality of who he was. She didn't get to know the more complex sides of his character; she has never really heard anything about his sexuality or what he was like in relationships. She has an idealised picture of her father. This means that her frustration around the men in her life is built on a background accusation that they are not as good as someone whose true nature she never knew.

A central theme of therapy for Miriam has been realising that she could imagine ways in which her father was far from perfect, without feeling that this is being unfair to him or damaging to her loyalty to the good things she remembers. He could have been (and certainly was) both a very good father and a very ordinarily flawed and muddled man. Had he lived, she would inevitably have clashed with him in lots of ways, found him annoying, embarrassing and disappointing – because these are standard parts of growing up. Miriam realises the cost of not having had an adolescence around her father.

Although childhood may be long over, the tendency to 'split' those close to us is always there. We can find it hard to accept that the same person might be very nice and good in some ways and very disappointing in others. The bad version can appear to destroy the good one, although these are just different and connected aspects of one complex human being.

In therapy, Miriam has been reconsidering her past relationships. The men she is so good at mocking were indeed annoying in certain ways, but they were also (to varying degrees) kind, intelligent, generous, tender and hard-working. And they were all fascinated by her. She was disturbed by flaws that need not have been fatal. She realises that there will be something wrong with whoever she is with, not because she has 'crazy taste in men' but because everyone is odd and frustrating when we get to know them well.

Recently Miriam has become closer to her grandmother – her father's mother. Her grandmother has fleshed out the picture of her son in loving, but not always flattering, ways. Miriam has been able to accept that her father could be moody, sly, underhand and at times irresponsible about money. He was far from perfect – and yet he was lovely.

Now Miriam has started going out with a man who, she admits, she wasn't mad about at first. His taste in clothes leaves something to be desired; he talks too much about his work; she doesn't like all his friends. But they have had some very interesting weekends together and she likes the way he warmly makes fun of her more eccentric sides. He's also hit it off with her grandmother.

Anxious and avoidant attachment

Depending on what happened when we were growing up, many of us tend as adults to have a bias towards either an anxious or an avoidant way of behaving in relationships. With an anxious pattern of being around our lovers, when there is difficulty we may grow officious, procedural and controlling over small matters of domestic routine. We feel our partners are escaping us emotionally, but rather than admitting to our sense of loss and our fear, we respond by trying to pin them down administratively. We get unduly cross when they are eight minutes late; we chastise them for not having done certain chores; we ask them strictly if they have completed a task they had vaguely agreed to undertake. All this rather than admit the underlying, poignant emotional truth: 'I'm worried that I don't matter to you...'

Jayathri (a GP) and Arun (who works in IT) have been together for four years. Eighteen months ago, they bought a house together with the idea that they might start a family one day. But increasingly they've been arguing a lot. The rancour can last for days. There are sulks, bitterness and a bad atmosphere that refuses to budge. They both regret it, but are at a loss as to what to do. They have come for couples therapy.

In the first session, Jayathri complains that Arun is appallingly unreliable: he says he'll pick up the dry cleaning, and then not actually do so; or when they've arranged to go out to dinner, he'll tell her at the last minute that he'll be 15 minutes late. At home she finds it maddening when Arun checks his phone just when she's trying to tell him something important about a food delivery or his mother.

When she complains, to make matters worse, he doesn't say anything. He just looks into the middle distance, then sneaks off to do some computer thing in the room upstairs. It seriously annoys her that he can't even speak. Almost in tears, she describes how he 'tunes out' and how she ends up having to take charge of everything herself.

Avoidant attachment is a pattern of relating to lovers whereby, when there is difficulty, we grow unusually cold and distant, and deny our need for anyone. We may desperately want to communicate, to be reassured and to get our point across, but feel so unconfident that we may be unheard or unwanted that we disguise our need behind a façade of indifference. Rather than stay present and struggle towards closeness, we say that we're busy, we pretend our thoughts are elsewhere, we become sarcastic and dry; we imply that a need for reassurance would be the last thing on our minds.

Visibly agitated, Arun says he often feels he would rather be on his own than have his girlfriend nagging him. Why can't she just be kind? He resents the way she's so bossy and tries to direct what he does with his phone. The worst thing is when Jayathri stands on the landing and shouts at him through the door of his study. She can go on for half an hour or more. Arun is normally quite reserved during this tirade, but it eventually makes him furious. Sometimes he'll scream at her to 'fucking leave me alone', and then return apparently calmly to his computer.

Patterns of attachment are not easy to budge, but it is hugely beneficial to understand which one we might have so as better to warn those we love, and apologise after the storm.

Arun grew up in a lively, busy family; his parents (originally from India) were – and still are – academics, often at conferences and preoccupied by work. When he was a child, they entertained a lot at home; no one minded if he left the grown-ups having long, loud conversations around the dining table and went to watch television in his bedroom.

On one occasion he wasn't feeling very well and went down to the kitchen to tell his mother. She gave him a hug, but didn't stop talking to her friends. He felt his parents weren't very bothered about what was happening at school. They were so taken up with teaching students it was as if they didn't think anything really mattered 'until you went to university'. When he was fourteen, he tentatively tried to tell his father there was a girl he was interested in and his father (Arun rolls his eyes as he says this) went off into a kind of lecture about 'the Western Myth of Romantic Love'. In that kind of setting, it was pretty pointless trying to explain very much.

The crucible of avoidant attachment is the child's sense that a parental figure lacks concern. To seek closeness is to guarantee humiliation. The child gives up on hoping for warmth and closeness; they withdraw and bury their longing for affection so as to avoid any rebuff. They learn not to care whether anyone says anything sweet or tender; they close down any interest in gentle signs of reassurance or playful gestures of affection. They feel cautious and uneasy around the expression of emotion, whether in themselves or by others. They may find this an advantage in a professional environment, but in relationships they can instinctively push away a partner who seeks a deeper connection. At their core, they are not without emotional needs, but they have, over the years, committed a lot of resources to coming across this way.

For her part, Jayathri spent her childhood in Sri Lanka, where her family were involved in a number of businesses, mainly around textiles and construction. It was a volatile and chaotic upbringing; her parents could be bountiful and warm one day and cold and frightening the next; there was a huge falling out across their extended family over an inheritance. Twice, when she was seven and then nine, she had to abruptly change schools for reasons that were never made clear to her. When she was fifteen, she was sent to a school in England. She was very lonely at first but later did well, winning prizes in Biology and Chemistry: 'I had to pull myself together and just get on with it.'

Across sessions, without ever being direct, the couples therapist gets Arun and Jayathri to focus on the underlying concepts of 'anxious' and 'avoidant' relationship styles. As a child, Arun had developed an avoidant strategy to cope with his parents' lack of attention. When he goes off to his room now, it's not because he doesn't care but because he feels he'll never be listened to and that he can't explain anything to another person. Technology appeals to him because it's automatically responsive; it won't ask him to account for himself or shout when there's a distracted look in his eyes.

Jayathri's anxious pattern of behaviour stems from her childhood way of coping with family relationships that she felt were unstable and untrustworthy. She resorted to imposing external order as a way of coping with a sense of emotional flux. When she feels lonely or sad, her instinct is to try to micromanage. It is not that she's essentially domineering: when she says 'turn off your phone' or 'take the rubbish out now, how many times do I have to ask you?', it is her garbled way of trying to say 'I need you and I want to be close to you.'

When we are anxious in relationships, we can't (we believe) force the partner to be generous and warm. We can't force them to want us (even if we haven't asked them to). The goal isn't really to be in charge all the time; it's just that we can't admit to our terror at how much we need the other. A tragic cycle then unfolds. We become shrill and unpleasant. To the other person, it feels as if we can't possibly love them anymore. Yet the truth is we do: we just fear too much that they don't love us. As a final recourse, we may ward off our vulnerability by denigrating the person who eludes us. We pick up on their weaknesses and complain about their extensive shortcomings. Anything rather than ask the question that so much disturbs us: does this person love me? Yet, if this harsh, graceless, anxious behaviour could be understood for what it is, it would be revealed not as a rejection, but as a strangely distorted – yet very real and touching – plea for tenderness.

Initially, these interpretations of their own and each other's behaviour felt very alien to Arun and Jayathri. But after several months of weekly sessions together, the true meaning of their behaviour to one another is starting to come into view.

Arun is learning to say 'I feel you're not listening and that makes me feel like running away from the terror of not being heard' rather than retreat to his 'cave'. Jayathri can sometimes say 'I'm feeling overwhelmed and I'm worried you don't love me' rather than 'we're meeting Karen and David at 7.30 so you'll need to be back by 6.50 at the latest; the taxi is at 7.15 and you should wear the dark blue shirt.'

They still squabble quite often and things are far from perfect, but the tensions tend to get resolved much more quickly; they can sometimes calm down after a few minutes. They are more accepting of their needs. Jayathri can admit that Arun is more solitary than she is, and it's not a rejection of her. Arun can see that Jayathri likes to plan and organise and that this doesn't have to be seen as an attack on him. It is not a perfect match – there are still tensions – but on the whole they are much more comfortable with their life together.

V
Conclusion

Our suspicions
of therapy

It is easy, and even important for a while, to be suspicious of therapy. Our doubts tend to cluster in five main areas.

1. Therapy is only for the crazy

A widespread belief implies that therapy is a resource reserved for the mad. Only on the basis of having drastically failed as a human being would we ever consider going to 'see someone'.

But therapy is merely a sophisticated response to the very normal distresses of the human condition. Everyone is a touch crazy, if we define craziness as the inevitable result of having been confronted at too young an age with problems too large and too threatening to be dealt with optimally and thereby acquiring coping strategies – of which we're largely ignorant – that hurt us and others and limit our capacities for fulfilment. In this specific sense, we are all mad and therefore prime candidates for assistance of some kind. What qualifies us for therapy is not a unique stain on our identity; it is membership of the human race.

Therapy can usefully be compared with certain traditional religious practices, such as atonement or confession, that were also interpreted as universally relevant rather than set aside for a few exceptionally persistent sinners. Every moderately self-aware and modest person was presumed to understand that they had done things they regretted and knew of ways they might improve. Participating in religious rituals was hence no marker of extreme depravity; it was, as therapy continues to be, an appropriate response to one's allotted share of frailty and confusion.

2. Therapy is self-indulgent

It is tempting to declare an activity one is suspicious of a 'luxury'. Depending on the perspective, it can be deemed a 'luxury' to read all the time, exercise every day, bake one's own bread or buy an Italian car. The term 'luxury' is simply an insult for what one has no interest in rather than a category defined by cost.

Psychotherapy is routinely accused of being a self-indulgence by people who see nothing especially luxurious about going on a skiing holiday or hiring a personal trainer. The underlying worry seems to be that, by talking closely about ourselves once a week or more, our personalities are at risk of growing dangerously egoistic. The interest of the therapist within the consulting room may, the assumption goes, breed a belief that everyone can and should find moments of our psychological history as compelling as they proved in therapy. But this is to misunderstand the origins of egoism, which lie not in excessive intelligent attention but in neglect. Therapy is unlikely to make us less interested in the lives of others; the greater probability is that it will free us from certain inner torments that have to date prevented us from participating fully in the experiences of those around us.

Another worry is that therapy is a costly replacement for friendship, and indicates a failure to develop the empathy and kindness involved in making true friends. But this apparent defence of friendship fails to acknowledge the rules and codes of conduct that govern the institution. We cannot expect an ordinary friend to listen with huge intelligence, care and persistence on a weekly basis to our secret troubles, put their own needs to one side and formulate subtle interpretations of our histories dating back to early childhood. This would be as ambitious, and as unattuned to the legitimacy of professional skill, as wishing that a friend could fly us to another country or perform open heart surgery on us simply on the basis that they like us. It is appropriately respectful of friendship to know all that it cannot be and do.

3. Therapy robs us of dignity

Therapy works with ideas that challenge notions of adult dignity. Through its processes, we are led to contemplate some distinctly awkward possibilities: that a lot of what we are today is motivated by processes we have in common with a bewildered three-year-old; that in a sense we haven't matured very much in many decades.

The solution to the apparently dispiriting aspect of this thesis is to reconfigure what it might mean to be, in certain areas, 'younger' than our biological age. To remain a bewildering mixture of an adult and a wounded child is no rare or insulting proposition. We shouldn't fear it as a dark possibility to be contemplated in the shadows, but rather embraced in the daylight with good humour and wry self-deprecation. We are never quite done with the business of growing up.

4. Therapy lacks confidence

Some of our suspicions of therapy can be traced back to the way it looks and feels. We may understandably associate it with some slightly odd-sounding unkempt figures who practise it from attics or pokey basement rooms. They might turn up to a cocktail party wearing sandals; they can seem devoid of any aura of prestige or confidence. This is legitimately disconcerting. It is natural to hope to see outward signs of success before we entrust our inner lives, especially their more broken and failed parts, to another person. But this is an accident of history rather than a structural problem of therapy. The shabby externals indicate that the practice has not yet reached its full stature, and that doing so might involve smartening up a bit.

5. Therapy will change everything

The last but most acute charge is that therapy over-promises. It can, unwisely, be presented as the key to transforming us into rich, invincible achievers who will triumph in love and work. Such inflated promises rightly invite doubt. But ultimately they are not a true reflection of what therapy hopes to do for us. Its authentic aim is more

111

limited: to assist us in the task of becoming slightly more mature, slightly less compulsive and occasionally more self-aware participants in the human drama. Therapy cannot annul the essential pains of existence, but it can equip us to cope with them with a touch more courage and dignity.

How therapy
might change us

What sort of person might we be after therapy, if the process were to go as well as could be hoped?

We will still quite often be unhappy. People will continue to misunderstand us; we'll meet with opposition; there will still be things that will be out of reach; success will come to people who don't appear to deserve it, and much that is good about us won't be fully appreciated by others. We will still have to compete with and submit to the judgement of others; we will still be lonely sometimes; and therapy won't stop us falling ill, dying and watching the people we love pass away. Therapy can't make life better than it truly is.

However, with these caveats in place, there are still substantial benefits that therapy can bring us.

1. We will have slightly more freedom

A key feature of the defences we build up against our primal wound is that they are rigid and limit our room for manoeuvre. For example, we may have a distinctive but unfortunate type that we go for in love; or we can't be touched in certain places; or we have to be constantly cynical or else insistently jolly. Our sense of who we are allowed to be and what we can do is held prisoner by the shocks of the past.

The more we understand the original challenges and the logic of our responses to them, the more we can take a risk of deviating from whom we once felt we had to be to survive. Perhaps we can, after all, afford to hope; or to go on top, or to spend some time alone, or to try a new job.

We realise that what we had believed to be our inherent personality was just a position we had crouched into to deal with the prevailing atmosphere. Having taken a measure of the true present situation, we may accept that there could be other, sufficiently safe, ways for us to be.

2. We can be readier to explain ourselves

We had learnt to be ashamed and silent. But the therapist's kindness and attention encourages us to be less disgusted by ourselves and furtive around our needs. Having once voiced our deeper fears and wishes, they can become slightly easier to bring up again with someone else. There may be an alternative to silence.

With a greater sense of our right to exist, we may become better at articulating how it feels to be us. Instead of just resenting another person's criticism, we might explain why we believe they have been unjust to us. If we are upset by our partner, we don't don't need to accuse them of evil and flee the house. Rather than escape, we will know to explain how (perhaps strangely) sensitive we are and how much reassurance we need to feel secure in their affection. Instead of trying to pretend that nothing is ever our fault, we can offer a candid explanation of our limitations and commit to trying to do better going forward.

3. We can be more compassionate

In the course of therapy, we will realise how much we were let down by certain people in the past. A natural response might be blame. But the eventual, mature reaction (building on an understanding of how our own flaws arose) will be to interpret their harmful behaviour as a consequence of their own disturbance. The people who caused our primal wound almost invariably didn't mean to do so; they were themselves hurt and struggling to endure.

The people
who caused
our primal
wound almost
invariably
didn't mean to
do so.

We can develop a sad but more compassionate picture of a world in which sorrows and anxieties are blindly passed down the generations. The insight isn't only true to experience; holding it in mind will mean there is less to fear. Those who wounded us were not superior, impressive beings who knew our special weaknesses and justly targeted them. They were themselves highly frantic, damaged creatures trying their best to cope with the litany of private sorrows to which every life condemns us.

In these ways, therapy will have done some of its most important work.

The School of Life offers psychotherapy, online and in person, all around the world. For more, please see:

www.theschooloflife.com/therapy

The School of Life is dedicated to developing emotional intelligence – believing that a range of our most persistent problems are created by a lack of self-understanding, compassion and communication. We operate from ten physical campuses around the world, including London, Amsterdam, Seoul and Melbourne. We produce films, run classes, offer therapy and make a range of psychological products. **The School of Life Press** publishes books on the most important issues of emotional life. Our titles are designed to entertain, educate, console and transform.

THESCHOOLOFLIFE.COM